Courageous Christianity

Courageous Christianity

Living A Life of Faith In a World That Desperately Needs Jesus

**DALE WITHERINGTON
(WITH DAN MONTAGUE)**

RESTORE MINNESOTA

ISBN: 979-8-89316-352-0 - Paperback
ISBN: 979-8-89316-351-3 - eBook

"Righteousness exalts a nation . . . . ."
Proverbs 14:34

Acknowledgments

First of all, let's give honor to Whom honor is most due, our Lord and Savior Jesus Christ. Community Action Teams are His idea and they are meant to be guided by His transforming power.

On the human plane, many thanks to our Senior Steward, Dan Montague, for his diligent and tireless efforts not only in leading our Community Action Team ministry but also for creating our Community Action Team Startup Manual.

And, from all of us at Restore Minnesota, our deepest thanks to those of you who asked, "What can we *do?*" *You* decided to storm the gates of hell via your local Community Action Team. *You* are the true heroes in the fight against unrighteousness in our land. We honor *you* for taking a stand for Jesus and showing "your backyards" what righteousness can look like in all seven Mission Fields of our culture!

Dedication

This book is dedicated to my life partner
of over 50 years, my wife, Sue.
You were born with a spirit of adventure
but you had no idea how that would
be tested in your journey with me as
your husband and best friend.
I couldn't have done any of this without
you. I love you. Forever.
Here's to the next 50 . . .

Table of Contents

Introduction

"We need an advisor. Will you help us?"

That was the question posed to me by a small group of Christian patriots after a friend of mine delivered to them his presentation on the Constitution of the United States. This group of 35–40 people called themselves the "Christian Constitutional Conservatives," and as one of the aspiring leaders put it, "in that order!"

What kind of help did they want?

It was May 2020. The whole world was locked down, but so-called "essential" businesses were still open. Do you remember the "essential" versus the "non-essential" distinction? Of course you do! The "essentials" were the big box stores, liquor stores, and bars. The "non-essential" businesses—the small, privately-owned, entrepreneurial businesses upon which our country and communities were built—were forced to close at the risk of ridiculous fines and overbearing government threats, including jail time.

Untold thousands of American families closed their doors or lost their businesses because of the terror tactics of certain state governors with their unconstitutional executive orders and their attorney general bullies.

One other sector was similarly affected by these over-reaching tyrants: the worship centers of America. The church in America was officially labeled by the government as "non-essential".

The sickening display by the government over the most foundational institution in America was only made worse by one thing: the church bought the lie and closed its doors.

OK, I get it. We didn't know what we were dealing with, so for some it made sense to lock 'em down for a couple of weeks while the government and medical community "flattened the curve". But, after a couple of weeks, what happened? Many churches remained masked, temperature-checked at the door, and distanced once inside.

Churches were instructed not to sing so that the moisture filling the atmosphere would not infect other worshipers. One pastor made her choir quit their Sunday morning rehearsal an hour early so the moisture droplets from singing would have a chance to hit the floor and dry before other congregants entered and were exposed to the COVID virus.

People lived in fear, even in the church. A church living in fear proved the government right in one sense—a fearful church is a non-essential church. Jesus did not suffer and die to build a fearful church. Unfortunately, at just the moment when the church could have shined the brightest, it turned out the lights and went online. Many of those watching from home still haven't returned.

So, here I was with a small group of people in central Minnesota from five or six Protestant and Catholic churches telling me they felt like they had to *do* something, but didn't know *what*. They didn't know where to turn for assistance. Their pastors and churches wouldn't help. On the one hand, they were being told by their spiritual leaders that they must obey the government according to Romans 13. On the other hand, they were told that if they were really loving others like Jesus told them to love, they'd shut up, mask up, and quit whining about getting an unproven, untested, so-called "vaccine". They were trapped between the proverbial rock and a hard place.

These men and women loved Jesus, their pastors, their churches, and their neighbors. They knew inherently that the teachings they were receiving about Romans 13 were incorrect, but they didn't know in what way. They believed with all of their being that their medical freedom was being denied, and the thought of having an unproven "vaccine" injected into their bodies was just not acceptable or responsible. Some were chastised by family and friends. Some were threatened. Some were business owners who lost customers. Churches lost congregants. Families separated. Livelihoods were lost. Spiritual leadership was neutered.

These Christian Constitutional Conservatives were courageous Christian patriots who loved God, loved their country, and loved their neighbors. They believed what we are now finding out to be true: we were sold a lie. These people understood that love is not really love if it is not connected with truth. They understood that a lie cloaked with the appearance of compassion is not compassion. It is a lie.

Love without truth is not love. "Compassionate" lying is really manipulation. And, throughout 2020, lying and manipulation was the name of the game. But, it sure made some people and some big businesses a lot of money.

The Lord is clear. He will not be mocked. Liars and manipulators will pay in the end. Pray for them. Without genuine repentance, their end is ugly.

I agreed to drive the three hour round trip for a couple of weeks to watch, listen, and determine if I could offer the assistance for which they asked. A couple of weeks turned into a month, and one month into several. My wife and I grew to love those people, and we made the weekly trip for over a year, even in the midst of a Minnesota winter, to help these Christian Constitutional Conservatives develop what we all agreed would be a duplicatable model for what we now call Community Action Teams, or CATs.

We developed and live by a mission statement that is unbending. We recognized five pillars that we will not break. We understood the long-range goal of developing at least one CAT in each of Minnesota's 87 counties, and perhaps at least one in every county in the USA. This was not some marketing vision. It was our understanding of a mandate from our Lord Jesus. We knew we were being called to *re-form the church to transform the world*.

This book is not only our story. It is how you, too, can gain influence in your community through the establishment of godly leadership. It is a path for never being canceled or deemed non-essential ever again.

It is a path for the restoration of righteousness in America.

Intervention

In June of 2012, I was accepted by a national ministry to become a non-political, non-partisan chaplain to elected state leaders, their families, and staff in the state of Minnesota.

I often joke about the ideal of being non-political and non-partisan lasting about 27 seconds.

As I underwent a baptism of fire in the halls of Minnesota politics, I quickly discovered much of the legislation being debated was more about issues of the Bible than issues of government. Apparently, in Minnesota, the left-leaning government felt particularly comfortable dictating to the church what was "legal" regarding certain historical doctrines of the Christian faith, while at the same time telling the church to stay out of government and politics due to the "separation of church and state". In fact, four bits of legislation that passed early in my tenure directly correlated with 18 of the 45 Goals of the American Communist Party as shared in our nation's Congress, January 10, 1963, to turn America into a godless, communist country.

It was one-sided hypocrisy at best and tyrannical bullying at worst.

Before I go further, allow me to clarify that I am not here to promote any political party. I have learned to be an equal opportunity offender of both major parties.

In Minnesota, for instance, the Republican *party* (as opposed to individual Republican candidates and officials), is a dumpster fire. The strength of the party is the value of independence. The weakness of the party is the value of independence. There are certain factions in the party who think they "own" their precincts and BPOUs (Basic Political Organization Units). The lack of unity or sense of common mission is appalling, and yet there was a recent "Unity" event to promote unity between Democrats and Republicans.

What?!

On the other hand, the Democrat Party is Chernobyl. There are those who *insist* it be called the *Democratic* Party but, in my decade-plus experience ministering at the Capitol, it is anything *but* democratic. This is the party that has become the bullying, threatening, damning culture of death, of the destruction of children and families, and of the intentional dismantling of American values. As of this writing, the party is led by communists (as demonstrated by their policies) and the self-proclaimed "Queer Caucus". They go out of their way to violate the Constitution of both the United States and Minnesota to push their anti-American, God-mocking, Marxist, and sexual-indoctrination agenda.

Marx said his two goals were to dethrone God and destroy capitalism. A self-proclaimed transgender Minnesota state representative recently said it was his mission to dismantle organized religion. Another state rep called people of faith—Christians, Jews and Muslims—disgusting, and repeated it in a singular committee meeting multiple times.

But, God will not be mocked. In fact, He will intervene.

The way He intervened for me was in a completely unexpected manner that shattered my personal theological boxes. I was completely unprepared for what God did *in* me and it rattled me to my core. It also completely changed the trajectory of my life and ministry.

But First,
Some Necessary History

Like many of us, I grew up well-loved, but steeped in an environment of dysfunction and marital brokenness. My last name came from being adopted by my third dad. My family doesn't have a family tree—we have a family bush.

We were not a particularly religious family, although my mother and grandmother made sure I said my prayers each night before bedtime. Those two prayers were the traditionally-called "Lord's Prayer" and the "Now I Lay Me Down to Sleep" prayer. I say "traditionally-called" because I don't personally refer to "The Lord's Prayer" in a traditional manner. I think what we call "The Lord's Prayer" is really the disciple's prayer, since it was a model that Jesus taught His disciples to pray, at their request. If I want "The Lord's Prayer," I go to John 17. The reason I think this is because the Matthew prayer teaches the disciples the principles of prayer. In John 17 we find Jesus Himself praying. That's why I call John 17 "The Lord's Prayer".

How about that "Now I Lay Me Down to Sleep Prayer"? I'm not sure it's a good idea to teach your four year-old "if I should die before I wake" if you ever want him or her to actually go to sleep without endless glasses of water and trips to the bathroom!

But I digress.

I was baptized as an infant in the Greek Orthodox Church, first heard the gospel in a kindergarten Sunday School class at a Lutheran Church, made a personal commitment to Christ on the pitcher's mound at Anaheim Stadium (the Big "A") because of some Baptist friends, and ended up at a Swedish Baptist college where I met and married a Presbyterian. Truth be told, she actually attended a Baptist church for a couple of years before returning to her Presbyterian church, so I guess I married a Bapterian.

After graduating from our little Swedish Baptist seminary, I accepted a position and was ordained in a large independent Baptist Church. That was in the early 1980s. By the time I started working at the Capitol, we had become members in a mildly charismatic "Word of Faith" church, much to the chagrin and confusion of my more traditionally-minded evangelical friends.

I have ministered and taught in over 20 different denominational groups about evangelism, discipleship, and the uniqueness of Jesus Christ. My wife says I became so non-denominational I was in danger of creating a denomination out of non-denominationalism. I've assured her others have already beaten me to it.

I shared all that to tell you something you might have a hard time believing. Keep reading to see what I mean.

Garlic from Heaven

This will be the chapter where I either lose you or lock you in. For those of you about to leave, thanks for hanging in there long enough to get this story. You're here now, so you might as well stick around!

It is not merely *a* story. It is *my* story, and my wife and I, as well as a lot of our ministry partners, have staked our lives and ministry on this personal testimony.

The date was May 20, 2013. It was the last night of my first legislative session in St. Paul. More than that, it was the end of our legislative biennium. The gavel needed to fall by 11:59 p.m. to fulfill the constitutional guidelines for the ending of a legislative session. Everything I'm about to tell you happened between 11:55 and 11:59 p.m.

My wife and I were in the gallery of the Senate chambers to quietly pray for our senators as they were wrapping things up. The only other person in the gallery was the Sergeant-at-Arms. It was nearly midnight.

Since my wife and I were the only civilians present, the Sergeant-at-Arms didn't mind that we were standing up while praying. My wife paced quietly while I stood at the gallery's brass rail, which protected me from a fall to the Senate floor about 15 or so feet below.

I was quietly praying with my eyes open so I could see those for whom I was praying. As I looked around the room, I had an experience that completely contradicted anything I had ever learned in college or seminary.

The Senate chamber, like many of the rooms in the Minnesota Capitol building, is stunningly beautiful. It is easy to take this beauty for granted when it is your workspace and, in many instances, the venue for your political battles.

About 150 feet from where I was standing at the rail was the section of the Senate chamber kitty-corner from me. There I caught something in my peripheral vision, floating in the air at eye level, about 2o feet above the floor.

Descending out of heaven was a bulb of garlic, just like the kind you would buy from the produce section of your local grocery store. It freaked me out. My theological boxes allowed for floating ax heads in a river (2 Kings 6:6), but they did not allow for bulbs of garlic descending out of heaven. So I did what every brave warrior for the Lord would do.

I closed my eyes.

I'm not sure what I thought closing my eyes would do, but it didn't matter. Even with my eyes closed, I saw and watched that bulb of garlic float across the room toward me. I *watched it* and *felt it* go through my sternum, enter my heart and slide down into my belly, where it stopped.

At that point, all I could do was say, "OK, Lord. What is this?"

The non-audible but clear voice of the Lord answered, "Restore Minnesota."

I responded to Him, "Great! What does that mean? And, as long as we're at it, it's 2013. America is in a mess. Why don't we restore America?"

He replied, "I've got America. You've got Minnesota."

Then He and the vision were gone.

To say I was stunned is an understatement.

Immediately, I walked over to my wife and interrupted her prayers so I could tell her what I had experienced. I prefaced my remarks by telling her I needed to tell her what happened because I would be telling this story for the rest of my life, and I didn't want to forget any details. As if that was a possibility! I also told her that when I shared the story going forward, there would be many who would simply think I'm looney tunes.

She listened closely until I was done, then looked me in the eyes the way only a wife can look at her husband. Then she asked, "So … why garlic?"

My stunned response was a somewhat animated, "I don't know. Do you realize what just happened to me?!"

It was a very quiet 45-minute ride home. My wife and I have different memories of the timing of what happened after we got home, but we agree on this: we had to discover the significance of garlic. I knew I wouldn't sleep well until I understood what it meant to "Restore Minnesota".

Confirmation

Our research on garlic yielded two items that carried spiritual significance for me. First, we learned that garlic purifies the heart. The Bible has a lot to say about the need for the heart to be purified, cleansed, made new, even replaced (see Ezekiel 36:22-28). The Bible also tells us that God was looking for a man after His own heart and used King David as the example (1 Sam. 13:14; Acts 13:22).

The idea of "consecration" fits as well, meaning a preparation or setting apart for God's service. It took me a while, but after focusing on the fact that the garlic had stopped in my belly and the Lord instructed me to "restore Minnesota," He started by having the garlic enter *my* heart. This was a new moment of consecration for me. It opened a new dimension of my calling in ministry.

Another quality of garlic is that it is known to kill viruses. My theological mind immediately went to the thought that sin is a spiritual virus. A new heart and a sin-killing (virus-killing) herb is a powerful picture.

My wife, Sue, was a bit more pragmatic at the time, which is somewhat unusual since she is often more spiritually sensitive. She pointed out that she had a wart on her hand and wasn't sure what process she wanted to follow to remove it. She said that warts were caused by viruses, and a light bulb came on in her mind. What if...?

Before going to bed that night, Sue made a paste out of the fresh garlic we had in our kitchen. She put the paste on the wart, wrapped a bandage around it and went to bed. When she got up in the morning, she took the bandage off and ... voila! The wart came off, root and all. It has not returned since May 2013.

This is the point in the story when many people I speak to start praising God. It's fun to hear. I, too, praised God for taking care of this "major medical issue" for my wife.

But, I had to ask the Lord one major question: "What does removing a wart from my wife's hand have to do with restoring Minnesota?"

Sometimes I'm a little slow in receiving confirmation from the Lord, and what happened next took us deeper into discovery.

Attacking Our Children, Families and Homes

I received a phone call inviting me to what I thought was a gathering of prominent political leaders in Minnesota. I thought it would be wise to attend and make some meaningful connections that might open doors for future ministry.

My wife and I never could have expected what we walked into.

The late Dr. Judith Resiman, an attorney for Mat Staver's Liberty Counsel, had been invited to give us an eight-hour seminar on a piece of legislation that she said would pass the Minnesota legislature in 2014 unless we did something to stop it. It really caught us off-guard.

Dr. Resiman told us she had just returned from a European country that had passed this same legislation. She met with the president of that country to tell him they had just passed the most pornographic school curriculum in the history of his nation. When she showed him the content of the main text, he immediately called for an emergency meeting of his cabinet. That led to an immediate meeting of their country's legislature.

They reviewed Dr. Reisman's information and voted to repeal their legislation. They did not want their children corrupted with a curriculum the FBI in America labeled as child pornography.

Dr. Reisman told us that a warden at a maximum security prison in California had banned that book from the prison library because it was too pornographic for his maximum security inmates. The book in question is called *It's Perfectly Normal.* There is *nothing* normal about the content of that book, especially for ten year-old children.

Through drawings, not photos, it depicts a wide variety of sexual acts. Although the book was prohibited from being seen by hardened, incarcerated criminals, it was designed to "instruct" our children.

This book and many others that are much more sexually explicit are easily accessible in our public schools and libraries alike. Library associations and others who do not understand the law argue that it is a First Amendment right to shelve these books in schools and libraries. What they fail to realize is that the Department of Justice and the FBI have made it clear that child pornography is *not* a protected First Amendment right. And yet, attorneys for library associations keep using the First Amendment defense to keep these materials in the children's sections of the libraries, instead of moving them to the X-rated adult sections. Why is this?

Furthermore, why are Minnesota's public schools exempt from obscenity laws? Is it to help the perpetrators who want to abuse our children? Are *your* public schools exempt from obscenity laws? You might want to find out.

What kind of sick, evil people would want to expose our innocent children to the sexual experiences that God intended for enjoyment only between a husband and a wife, in the private intimacy of their marriage? Truth be told, some of these practices might not be intended by God for our enjoyment at all.

So, what was the bill in question? Its legal name was "The Minnesota Safe and Supportive School Act." It was advertised by a different moniker, "The Anti-Bullying Bill." It had nothing to do with bullying, except the bullying that was carried out by the pedophile-promoting lobbyists, the pedophile-protecting legislators, and their constituents who passed it.

We were told that this bill would be presented as unique to Minnesota, but we learned that the Minnesota bill came from a template being used by at least 15 other states. It was to begin a national theme of "anti-bullying" with the messaging that if you were *against* the bill you must be *for* bullying. The only bullying came from those whose real agenda was to do our children great sexual harm. If this is resonating with you, I suggest you read the book, *Stolen Honor, Stolen Innocence: How America was Betrayed by the Lies and Sexual Crimes of a Mad 'Scientist'* by the aforementioned Dr. Reisman.

After the seminar, about 35 of us gathered at the state capitol building in St. Paul and began a strategy to educate Minnesotans so we could stop the bill. A group of incredibly committed moms launched the Child Protection League (www.cplaction.com). Several of us traveled the state speaking to churches, civic groups, and any number of organizations who would hear us out. We told them that if the bill passed, the results would include:

- Men wanting access to women's public bathrooms.
- Boys wanting to play sports on girls teams, as well as dressing and showering with the girls. If the sports team was an overnight traveling team, there would be four students to a hotel room, meaning if a boy was on the girls' team, a teenage girl would have to share a bed with a teenage boy.
- The beginning of something that would be called "transgenderism".
- Teachers becoming sexually active with students at an increasing rate.
- Pedophiles demanding the same civil rights protections enjoyed by gays and lesbians.

No matter where we went, people responded with the same verdict: It could never happen here.

Unfortunately, the bill passed in 2014. More unfortunately, everything we said would happen, happened. Things changed at a much greater rate than we could have imagined, and this ideology dominates civil rights and political agendas today. Who would have thought in 2014 that by 2024 we'd be told to accept not only a vast variety of genders and pronouns, but also to accept that it hurts the feelings of pedophiles to be identified as such. They prefer the euphemistic "Minor Attracted Adults". Doesn't that make you feel better?

We discovered that one of the leading organizations nationwide for pushing this sexual agenda was Planned

Parenthood. A close second was the NEA, the National Education Association. The NEA is possibly the most evil union in America, in my opinion, with an agenda that has almost nothing to do with giving our children an education. That is, of course, unless you consider getting our children as sexually active as possible at ages younger than kindergarten is "age appropriate" education, and that if a girl gets pregnant, Planned Parenthood is there to provide the abortion.

Our children become little more than potential sexual money machines for the manipulative, evil leaders of Planned Parenthood, the NEA, and the human traffickers who think nothing of buying and selling children as sex slaves. It is big business, and they will attack anyone who tries to stop them.

They think they own our children.

I call B.S. on that. And I don't mean Bachelor of Science.

Since the so-called "Anti-Bullying Bill" passed, untold thousands of children have been forever scarred, harmed, and abused by evil adults with evil intent. Things have even degenerated into the mutilation of our children by allowing them "gender-affirming" surgeries when they think they have the wrong body for the gender they've been coerced into believing is their true identity. There's nothing "affirming" about any of this. It is destroying our children, our families, and our homes because, in some cases, if the parents of a minor child refuse to affirm their child's newly chosen gender or gender transition process, the government threatens to take the children from the home.

The inmates are running the asylum. America, a nation founded with a new form of government that is fit only for a moral and religious people, has descended into an abyss of moral and religious depravity.

Stay tuned, because this story gets crazier.

The Commies
are Coming! *Really*??

Nothing would have shut us down faster than to tell people the Communists were leading the charge in Minnesota politics in 2013 and 2014. The evidence was there.

In 1958, the book *The Naked Communist* was published. It was quoted in Congress in January of 1963 and revealed the 45 Goals of the Communist Party[1] for the takeover of America, which I provide in the appendix of this book. I first became aware of the 45 Goals after watching a video shared with me by the wife of one of our former state representatives. The award-winning movie by former state representative from Idaho, the Honorable Curtis Bowers, is called *Agenda.*

As I studied the movie, I was reminded of four bills that were passed in Minnesota in the 2013 and 2014

---

[1] Donald Boyd, Donalds's Thoughts blog, uploaded from *The Naked Communist*, the-naked-communist-goals-with-notes-and-highlights.pdf (donaldboyd.org).

legislative sessions that really caught my attention. Those four bills were:

1. Allowing same-sex "marriage".
2. The largest tax increase in the history of the State of Minnesota (which held true until 2023).
3. The unionizing of in-home private child care.
4. The aforementioned anti-bullying bill.

As I studied those bills, I began to see an intentional strategy by American-hating politicians, lobbyists, and organizations. It was like an octopus with a hundred tentacles. Cut one off and two grow back. Bring in a bill from one direction and toss in another seemingly unrelated bill from another direction. But one thing was clear as day. The four bills identified above corresponded directly to 18 of the 45 Goals.

Once I made this discovery, I couldn't start shouting, "The Commies are coming! The Commies are coming!" Nobody, and I mean nobody, was openly promoting Socialism/Communism/Marxism in 2013.

Thank God for Bernie Sanders and his attempt to run for President in 2016. Bernie, followed by Maxine Waters and others, brought the socialist agenda into the light. They began the now popular Democratic Socialist movement in America, a political philosophy that has failed 100 percent, every time it has been tried around the world. Talk about an oxymoron! When has *anything* socialist had any vestiges of being democratic? Never, unless you like a dictator-led mob rule.

But when you take this failed philosophy, tie it to the public school system and mandate the teaching of Marxism as a requirement for getting and keeping a teacher's license, you begin to understand why America's students are being indoctrinated and groomed by educational foundations that are intended to tear down our nation. This was done, by the way, in 2023 in Minnesota, when an administrative judge approved the PELSB (Professional Educator's Licensing and Standards Board) revisions to teacher licensing even after 71 of 77 testifiers pointed out to the judge the Marxist and pornographic requirements built into the certifications.

In 2013, I couldn't say, "The Commies are coming!" but I could speak on the common thread of socialism, communism, and Marxism—atheism.

Read or re-read the 45 Goals included in the Appendix. You'll have a greater understanding of the agenda for taking down America.

What can thwart this effort?

Restoring Righteousness

When the Lord told me to "restore Minnesota," I discovered He was instructing me to "restore righteousness" in Minnesota. I still wasn't sure what that meant or how to do it.

The first questions I had to ask were, "When was Minnesota ever righteous in the first place? Doesn't restoring something imply that something that does not exist now used to exist sometime in the past? And, what exactly is my role in restoring righteousness? Isn't that something only God can do?"

As a pastor, I found my answers clearly taught in the Bible. The only time Minnesota or any other place on earth was considered by God to be "righteous" was in the original garden of Eden prior to the deception of Eve and the sin of Adam. So, to "restore righteousness" means God wants His people to be involved in the process of partnering with Him—restoring on earth the righteousness He had in mind when He created it. How do we at Restore Minnesota do that? We do it by adhering to our mission statement and staying true to our five foundational convictions or pillars.

Let's first address the idea of our mission statement.

Most of us are familiar with the idea of mission statements. Maybe you've been in the lobby of a corporate headquarters or a church where the "Mission Statement" is written on the wall for all to see. Maybe the company you work for has its own beautiful mission statement on a wall in your building.

The questions that often arise are:

1. Who is promoting the mission statement of our company on a daily or regular basis? and
2. How does my job fit in with the mission statement?

All too often there is a great disconnect. People tend not to know or understand the corporate mission or their role in it. It doesn't really matter as long as everyone continues to get their paychecks.

Please do not misunderstand or take offense to what I just said. It just seems to be the way the world works. Ask yourself how those two questions apply to your own work situation. Maybe you are among the blessed who can give more satisfactory answers to those questions.

I believe God is on a mission and, as I stated above, He is inviting us to become His partners in it. So, when it came to the idea of restoring righteousness in Minnesota, we created our understanding of what God was calling us to by writing our mission statement. I invite you to "steal" our mission statement and replace "Minnesota" with the name of your state.

Here is the Restore Minnesota Mission Statement:

"Restore Minnesota exists to restore righteousness in Minnesota by promoting biblical citizenship that educates, equips, empowers and encourages Holy Spirit-led engagement—county by county, community by community, family by family—resulting in spiritual and civic transformation based on the gospel, that is, the life, teachings, death and resurrection of the Lord Jesus Christ."

Ok, that's a mouthful. Let's break it down.

"Restore Minnesota exists to restore righteousness." This tells the world *why* we exist. It is the purpose that guides the mission. It also raises the questions, "What is righteousness?" and "What will my county, community, and family look like when we are all living righteously toward one another?"

Let's start by understanding that the concepts of justice, love, truth, integrity, honesty, charity, compassion, and devotion to the God of the Bible through the world's only Lord and Savior, namely, Jesus Christ, are only some of the meanings of the word "righteousness". Then we will begin to realize that the restoration of righteousness is a process to which we aspire but will never fully obtain until the Lord's return. Maybe that's what Jesus was teaching us in Luke 19:13 when He said to "occupy" or "engage in business" until He comes back. In other words, Jesus wants us to occupy our minds and engage in His mission of restoring righteousness.

We might ask, "How do we do that?"

In our mission statement, we say it is "by promoting biblical citizenship that educates, equips, empowers, and encourages Holy Spirit-led engagement ..."

The idea of biblical citizenship is gaining traction throughout the nation. In addition to our teachings on the topic, our friends Rick Green (www.PatriotAcademy.com), Keith Downey (www.bigskybiblicalcitizenship.com) and David Barton (www.WallBuilders.com) have put together great content to help Americans grasp the truth of our nation's heritage and the biblical basis for it. It's time for the church to understand that the idea of biblical citizenship comes from God. It is what He meant when Jesus gave us the mandate to "make disciples". More on that later.

Restore Minnesota is primarily an educational ministry, but we don't stop there. Education without application results in educational constipation. What good is all of our educational knowledge if we don't actually use it?

Consequently, real education happens only when there is a place to apply what we've learned. Real education is in the doing. It demonstrates the biblical principle that "faith without works is dead" (James 2:26).

This is why we call our teams "Community Action Teams" or CATs. Some say our motto is "Action is our middle name". In our case, the action must be based on accurate information with a targeted purpose. We must not be like the overanxious hunter who seems to operate on the philosophy of "Ready. FIRE. Aim."

Our recommendation manual for forming and operating a CAT is included at the end of this book. You can always reach out to us for personal assistance at our website, www.RestoreMN.org.

As of this writing, we have 15 CATs representing at least 17 counties. The objective is to place at least one CAT in every one of Minnesota's 87 counties. We have just scratched the surface. Even with 15 CATs and almost 2,000 on our email list, we can reach nearly 500,000 Minnesotans. There are 3,143 counties in the United States. Imagine if every one of them had a CAT!

To review, our organization exists to restore righteousness by promoting biblical citizenship county by county, community by community, and family by family. When this happens, a transformation takes place. That transformation begins in the individual who commits his or her life to following the Lordship of Jesus Christ in every area of life. This transformation is described throughout the New Testament.

A good place to start is Romans 12:1-2, "I appeal to you, therefore, brothers, by the mercies of God, to present your bodies as a living sacrifice, holy and acceptable to God, which is your spiritual worship. Do not be conformed to this world, but be transformed by the renewal of your mind, that by testing you may discern what is the will of God, what is good and acceptable and perfect."

Perhaps it would be a good idea to take some time now to read, think, and pray over those verses.

A transformed life impacts others through the indwelling of and powerful presence of the Holy Spirit. Transformed lives transform lives. When enough lives in a community are transformed, the community and its culture are transformed. When enough communities are transformed, a region or county and its culture is transformed. When enough counties are transformed, a state and its culture is transformed. When enough states are transformed, a nation and its culture is transformed.

Therefore, the call of the gospel is to transform nations (see Psalm 2).

How do we go about applying our mission statement? As I mentioned at the beginning of this chapter, we do so by utilizing five foundational convictions or pillars, which we will address in the next chapter.

The Five Pillars of an Effective Community Action Team (CAT)

A building is only as strong as its foundation. The same is true of any organization. It is especially true of a volunteer organization like Restore Minnesota. We don't "own" our CATs. We serve them. We are an affiliation of volunteers. The principle is true that the larger a volunteer organization becomes the more *fragile* it is, though that may seem contradictory.

Strength doesn't come from size. Nor does it come from the power of a personality. Strength comes from a commitment to Biblical truths. Here are ours. We recommend them to you for your prayerful consideration if you desire to start a CAT.

1. **Jesus Christ is Lord (Philippians 2:11)**

    Our first CAT was formed by nearly 40 people who came from six different churches, all located in the same general vicinity. These people represented a variety of Protestant and Catholic churches.

We agreed to unite under the banner "Jesus Christ is Lord" because, as an independent Baptist pastoral mentor of mine used to tell me, "If we cannot unite under the words 'Jesus is Lord,' we have much bigger problems than simply being in different denominations." In working with nearly 30 denominations, I have found this to be very sage advice.

This starting point allows us to function without any focus on denominations or denominationalism. We are neither here to promote or create any particular denomination, nor to tear them down.

In no particular order, see also: Romans 10:9, Revelation 19:16, 1 Corinthians 8:6, 1 Corinthians 12:3, 1 Peter 3:15, 2 Corinthians 13:14, and John 20:28 for more on "Jesus is Lord".

2. Jesus said He came to build his *ekklesia* (Matthew 16:18)

I find it rather unfortunate that most modern versions of the Bible translate the word *ekklesia* as "church". I say "unfortunate" because when we in the twenty-first century hear the word "church," we immediately think of a religious institution or organization. We think of Sunday morning worship services, small groups, and other things a local church does.

That was not the meaning of the word *ekklesia* in the first century when Jesus spoke it.

When Jesus said *ekklesia*, He was not referring to religion. Jesus was referring to government. *Ekklesia* in Jesus' day was a *political, governmental* term. It referred to the leaders of a community, not a religious organization.

The literal meaning of *ekklesia* comes from two Greek words roughly meaning "the called out ones". I find it unfortunate that the church has tended to interpret this as Jesus' instructions to separate itself from worldly affairs, to be "in the world but not of it". That is *not* what he meant.

Jesus did not come to earth to build a religion. He came to build a government over which He is Prophet, Priest, King, and Lord. He expects His people not only to participate in the governing of their communities and nations, but also to take part in leading them. Let's look at just a few verses here:

- Isaiah 9:6 – The *government* is on His shoulders. Here's where naysayers will say, "But Jesus said His kingdom is *not* of this world!" (John 18:36). This misses the point. Jesus did not equate His kingdom with earthly governments, so neither should we. However, Jesus did not mean for us to minimize His kingdom's influence on earthly governments.

- Proverbs 29:2 – "When the righteous increase, the people rejoice; But when the wicked rule, the people groan." This could only mean the church is responsible to raise righteous men and women, some of whom God will use in the governmental realm. Or, is the government the one part of culture that does not need Jesus?

○ Philippians 1:27 – This is one of my favorites because you have to dig a bit into the classical Greek understanding of the language. Many versions of the Bible quote this verse as a reminder to live in such a way that it demonstrates in a worthy manner the gospel of Jesus Christ. The Apostle Paul teaches this concept throughout his letters. However, the language he uses in Philippians is a bit different than elsewhere. The English Standard Version (ESV) identifies this difference by adding the footnote "Only behave as citizens worthy..."

In other words, Paul, who used his Jewish, Roman, and heavenly citizenships to advance the gospel, seems to be reminding the Philippians, who had been conquered by and annexed into the Roman Empire, that just as they were given new citizenship by Rome which was to be evident in everyday life, so also were they given a heavenly citizenship that was to be displayed on earth. This is emphasized by Paul's words in Philippians 3:20 that we Christians are "citizens of heaven," with the reminder in 2 Corinthians 5:20 that we have been called to be "ambassadors" to earth. Ambassadorship is a governmental term. However, if you go deeper into the original Greek language used by Paul and understand its meaning from a classical Greek perspective, it would not be much of a stretch to translate this verse: "Only do *politics* (emphasis mine) worthy of the gospel of Jesus Christ." That translation lines up extremely well with the true meaning of *ekklesia*.

Now imagine if we had churches who created mature disciples of Jesus, who He could call to become politicians and other governmental leaders, and who actually live out the meaning of *ekklesia*!

3. **Jesus said we should pray that God's kingdom would come and His will be done "on earth as it is in heaven" (Matthew 6:10).**

This is where we theologians can get into debates about kingdom of God theology. Let's not go there.

This is how we handle this piece of Scripture in our Restore Minnesota ministry:

Imagine if you and a group of your friends were living in heaven right now. Would it be a likely expectation that each of you would be fully obedient to the Lord's command, to love the Lord with all your heart, soul, mind and strength ... and your neighbor as yourself? (Mark 12:30, Luke 10:27, Matthew 22:37). Of course it would! Otherwise, it would not be heaven.

Also, in that same scenario, would it be a likely expectation that each of you would perfectly display the fruit of the Spirit—love, joy, peace, patience, kindness, goodness, faithfulness, gentleness, and self-control—as described in Galatians 5:22-23? Again, of course you would! Otherwise it would not be heaven.

What I'm illustrating here is the *culture* of heaven. It is that *culture* we are to bring into the earth. Jesus even provided the strategy to do that very thing.

4. **Jesus said He had been given *all* authority in heaven and on earth. As a result, He directed His *ekklesia*, His followers, to a task referred to as The Great Commission (Matthew 28:18-20).**

What is "the gospel"?

Most people reading this book understand that the words translated "the gospel" are from the Greek words meaning "good news". My question to you, the reader is, "What does the term 'gospel' mean to you?"

The answer for most, especially in the evangelical tradition, usually means something like, "Jesus was brutally beaten, tortured and put to death by one of the most horrific means of capital punishment known to mankind, namely, crucifixion. He took that beating and died *in our place*, and then was resurrected on the third day. By accepting Jesus as our Savior, our sins, which He paid for on the cross, could be forgiven and we can go to heaven when we die." We tend to restrict the word "gospel" to mean people being "saved".

I think the gospel, which means "good news," is that and a lot more.

If the gospel was really only about people getting saved so that when they die they would go to heaven, why wouldn't we help get people saved and then, once we "feel" assured they prayed the "sinner's prayer" sincerely enough to be saved, provide them with a pill or a bullet or some other means to help them get to heaven right away?

Clearly, I am overstating this to make a bigger point. Salvation is more than just "getting saved" so we can go to heaven when we die.

When Jesus came out of His 40 days in the wilderness following His baptism, His message of "good news" included:

- "Repent, for the kingdom of heaven is at hand" (Matthew 4:17).
- "The time is fulfilled, and the kingdom of God is at hand; repent and believe in the gospel" (Mark 1:15).
- "The Spirit of the Lord is upon me, because he has anointed me to proclaim good news to the poor. He has sent me to proclaim liberty to the captives and

recovering of sight to the blind, to set at liberty those who are oppressed, to proclaim the year of the Lord's favor" (Luke 4:18-19).

◦ "You must be born again ... of water and the Spirit" (John 3:1-21).

We might have been "born again" (John 3:3) but we are still in the process of being "saved" (1 Corinthians 1:18, 2 Corinthians 2:15).

These few selected verses illustrate Jesus' own teachings about the gospel, which included both going to heaven when one dies and being given an opportunity to live a new quality of life, a God-quality of life, in this present world.

For Jesus, the good news was all about His kingdom being brought to earth. It means Jesus giving us access on earth to God's way of doing things in all seven mission fields of culture. (More on the seven mission fields below.) Jesus wants us, His *ekklesia*, to access the kingdom's way of living on earth, the kingdom's way of doing things, and then to teach or disciple others to operate in the same way. It is His way of helping us fulfill His prayer that God's kingdom would come and God's will would be done *on earth as it is in heaven*. It is bringing the *culture* of heaven into the earth.

And just what is that culture?

We get so wrapped up in debating kingdom of God theology that we miss the bigger picture of what Jesus was trying to teach us.

Imagine for a moment that we are living in heaven right now. I think we would have at least two expectations:

1. We would all be perfectly obeying Jesus' greatest command to "love the Lord your God with all your heart and with all your soul and with all your mind" and to "love your neighbor as yourself" (Matthew 22:37–40).

2. We would also be perfectly displaying to one another the fruit of the Spirit in Galatians 5:22–23—love, joy, peace, patience, kindness, goodness, faithfulness, gentleness, and self-control.

If we were not perfectly experiencing and displaying at least these two things, we could not be in heaven, right? These would have to be perfectly experienced and displayed, or by definition we would not be in heaven.

These verses, then, illustrate the *culture* of heaven. It is this culture that Jesus wants His *ekklesia* to bring into the earth. That is what it means in practical terms for God's kingdom to come, and God's will be done *on earth as it is in heaven.*

Jesus even gave us the strategy for doing so, in His "Great Commission".

If churches followed the details of "The Great Commission" better, the result would be significant improvements in their ministries.

At Restore Minnesota, we refer to this as "Re-forming the church to transform the world."

This re-forming begins by understanding that the command of The Great Commission is not "Go" (Matthew 28) or "Preach" (Mark 16).

Since Mark's version in the sixteenth chapter of his book is captured fully in Matthew's version, let's do a deeper dive into Matthew 28:18–20.

"And Jesus came and said to them, 'All authority in heaven and on earth has been given to me. Go therefore and make disciples of all nations, baptizing them in the name of the Father and of the Son and of the Holy Spirit, teaching them to observe all that I have commanded you. And behold, I am with you always, to the end of the age.'"

It is unfortunate that too many of our English version Bibles, such as the ESV translation above, translate The Great Commission with the word "go" as if "go" is the main command. It is not.

The Greek word, *poeruthentes*, from which we get the word "go," is more accurately translated as "having gone" or "as you are going". It has the same construct and "ing" ending as the words translated to "baptizing" and "teaching".

Why the grammar lesson?

Its importance lies in the fact that a word with an "ing" ending cannot serve as the main verb or main course of action in a sentence. It cannot serve as the command. In this case, the three words ending with "ing" (going, baptizing, teaching) are *adverbs of manner* telling us *how* to accomplish the one main command of the verse. And what is that one command? It is to "make disciples of all nations".

Even the word translated as "nations" is more accurate as "all of the ethnicities or people groups of the world". Therefore, a better rendering of The Great Commission into English is:

"All authority in heaven and on earth has been given to Me. Therefore, *as you are going through your daily life***, make disciples of** *all the people groups of the world***, baptizing them in the name of the Father, and of the Son and of the Holy Spirit, teaching them to obey everything I have commanded you."**

This is where the reader may ask, "Why is this so important?"

I'm glad you asked!

For too long, the church in America has lost its relevance and effectiveness because we have focused on making converts instead of developing life-long disciples. We bought into a formula, called it "The Sinner's Prayer," and started counting the notches on our belts because we "got" another one to "pray the prayer".

I wonder how many of those who "prayed the prayer" are still walking with Jesus today?

Some argue it is God's job to provide the people who will disciple new converts. I disagree. When we help lead someone to Christ, our job is just beginning. It is our job to bring that person into a discipling relationship.

Unfortunately, that often doesn't happen because we have separated the function of evangelism from a life of discipleship. Churches hire "Evangelism" pastors and "Discipleship" pastors. By doing so, we create a false dichotomy. We forgot that the most effective evangelism is a changed life of discipleship, serving as a witness to the power of God.

I have walked with Jesus for over 50 years. I have been to countless events that led people to convert, that is, to give their lives to Jesus. I came to Christ at an event like that way back in 1969. However, I was fortunate to be connected to Christians who understood that the salvation prayer was not the end of my journey. It was a new beginning, a launching point into a new life. They understood that "getting a person saved" was not the end goal. Salvation is only the beginning.

The church in America needs a radical transformation. It begins by understanding the "gospel" is not about creating converts. The gospel is about creating disciples.

5. **Glorify God by completing your assigned task**

In talking with God the Father, Jesus said, "I glorified you on earth, having accomplished the work that You gave me to do" (John 17:4).

Have you ever thought about that for yourself? Have you ever said to the Lord something like, "Lord, I want to glorify You by completing the task You have given me to do. I only have one question: *What's the task?*"

Many credible sources have been quoted about the importance of knowing the two most important days in one's life. They tell us that the first most important day is the day you were born. They tell us the next most important day is the day you learn *why* you were born. It sounds brilliant, and they leave it at that, but I'm not satisfied. I believe there are not two, but four, most important days.

The third most important day, which falls on the heels of discovering *why* you were born, is the day you actually *decide to pursue* why you were born. But it is not enough simply to decide, which leads me to the fourth and perhaps most important day of all.

It is the day you actually *pursue* why you were born.

In the pursuit of your purpose you will begin the process of completing God's task that He assigned for you. How do you do that? Where do you begin?

At Restore Minnesota, we use a model I refer to as the "7 Mission Fields of Culture". Some refer to them as "Mountains of Culture". Some use "Spheres of Influence". There is no one right term.

If you are unfamiliar with the concept, and many Christians are, it goes back to the legendary story of a meeting Bill Bright, the founder of Cru (formerly Campus Crusade for Christ) and Loren Cunningham, the founder of Youth With a Mission (YWAM), had back in 1975. I was first exposed to the concept around 2001 by a great brother in the Lord, Os Hillman, the author of the very popular devotional for marketplace leaders, *Today God Is First*. It has been popularized by godly men such as Lance Wallnau, Johnny Enlow and Dr. John C. Maxwell. Maxwell is a man who had a tremendous personal mentoring impact on my life as a young pastor, one who has continued to mentor me and countless millions of others around the world over the decades through his writings and speaking.

The gist of the Seven Mountains is that all civilized societies have seven so-called mountains of culture, namely: Arts, Entertainment and the Media; Science and Technology; Business and Commerce; Government; Family; Education; and Religion. There is nothing specifically "scriptural" about these mountains, nor is there anything specifically "anti-scriptural" about them. They have changed a bit since 1975, and many others have created adaptations to the original concept. The idea we all seem to agree on is that it is a useful tool to help strategize and apply the biblical teachings of evangelism, discipleship, and biblical citizenship.

At Restore Minnesota, we choose "Mission Fields" not only to stay consistent with our mission statement and the first four pillars above, but also because a significant part of the Restore Minnesota ministry is in the Government mission field.

For those who question the idea of mixing Christianity with government and politics, please see "The Role of the Church in Government" in the Appendix.

Using the term "Mission Fields" accomplishes at least a few important objectives:

1. It reminds us that the primary job of Christian leaders, especially pastors, is "to equip the saints to do the work of ministry" (see Ephesians 4:11–16 ISV).

2. In light of #1 above, it also reminds us that there is no such thing as second-class Christians. It destroys the false dichotomy of the terms "clergy" and "laity," as if one is more important than the other. The terms are better understood as "roles," not "hierarchy". That is not to take away from the authority of Christian leaders as the shepherds and watchmen of their congregations, but it also doesn't make them more important, more spiritual, or more powerful than the individual members of their flocks. An earned title, such as Pastor, Reverend, or Doctor might be recognized as a title of respect,

but respect must still be earned. Titles do not make one member of the body of Christ superior to other people, whether they are members of the body or not.

3. It reminds us that Jesus Christ is Lord over *every* area of life on this earth, including Government, unless you are of the persuasion that our government systems and government leaders *do not* need Jesus. Again, I refer you to the Appendix and the topic "The Role of the Church in Government."

So, how does one apply the model of the "7 Mission Fields of Culture"?

To keep it simple, we suggest:

1. Identify the Mission Fields in which you already operate.

    Virtually everyone operates in more than one Mission Field. Take some time to write down the ones you are in and the roles you play. Acknowledge you are there because God placed you there, even if you believe you are in a Mission Field where He does not want you. More on that below.

2. Now ask God this most important question: "Lord, how can I be more effective where you have placed me?"

    Pray that prayer with sincerity over each of the mountains in which you have identified you are already operating.

Allow the Lord time to speak to your heart and write down what he impresses on you. This is where he will confirm where He really wants you and where He will reveal to you any mission field(s) you are working in which He has not assigned you. Imagine the freedom you will feel by pursuing only those areas in which you are assigned, and the release of burden you will have by leaving any mission field to which you are not assigned.

A word of caution is in order here. Please do not use a release from a particular mission field as an excuse not to operate as an effective witness for Christ when you do find yourself in the midst of a mission field that is not part of your purpose or calling. Remember that while there is a *specific* calling or purpose that only you can fill, there is a *general* calling for all Christians to participate in together.

Acts 1:8 tells us of that general calling: "But you will receive power when the Holy Spirit has come upon you, and you will be my witnesses in Jerusalem, and in all Judea and Samaria, and to the end of the earth."

In context, Jesus is preparing His followers for the coming of the Holy Spirit after Jesus' ascension into heaven. When I first learned this scripture as a new believer over 50 years ago, it was generally taught that we Christians would be witnesses for Christ in our home communities (Jerusalem), our general region (Judea), across racial divides (Samaria), and to every people group in the world (the end of the earth). In today's world, we grasp this concept as both an instruction to follow and a promise as yet unfulfilled. While it is believed by many world missions professionals that every people group on earth will be reached with the gospel of Jesus Christ by sometime in 2032 or 2033, and while many of the areas Jesus mentioned in Acts 1:8 have heard the gospel, try going from Israel into Judea today. It is fenced off, part of a major war zone. But, the Lord's promises and instructions will not be left unfulfilled. The doors will reopen. Pray for those Christians in Judea and Samaria whose lives are at risk as they use the wisdom of serpents and the harmlessness of doves to bring the light of the gospel deeper into areas of significant spiritual darkness.

In the meantime, we can apply Acts 1:8 in our own lives by understanding that *all* of us who call ourselves Christians are to be the "witnesses" of whom Jesus spoke. What does it mean to be a witness?

Let's first address what it does *not* mean. It does not mean "preacher" or "teacher". And, to the relief of the vast majority who do not have this particular spiritual gift, it does not mean "evangelist".

The literal meaning of the word translated "witnesses" is the word "martyrs". Isn't that a relief? We don't have to be evangelists. Instead, we are called to be martyrs. It almost makes you *want* to be an evangelist instead, right? What was Jesus *really* teaching us here?

Diving deeper, we see that Jesus is asking us, instructing us, to be testifiers on His behalf *no matter the potential or perceived cost.* What does that mean?

We gain a great insight here in 1 Peter 3:15. It says in the NIV, "But in your hearts revere Christ as Lord. Always be prepared to give an answer to everyone who asks you to give the reason for the hope that you have. But do this with gentleness and respect." Other versions replace "give an answer" with phrases like "give a defense". Biblehub.com is a good resource, as is the YouVersion Bible App, to get a variety of renderings on this and other passages of Scripture.

The question for each of us is, "What is *my* reason for believing? What is *my* testimony?"

Here is a simple exercise to assist you in telling your story, your testimony:

1. Take some time to write down what your life was like before you were introduced to Jesus. What was your life like before you committed your life to Him? There is no *right* answer. There is only *your* answer. This is *your* story.

2. Now write down how you were introduced to Jesus. What were the circumstances? Where were you? Who talked with you? How did you hear the gospel? What was going on in your life at the time that made you open to listening? Remember, this is *your* story.

3. Finally, write down how your life has changed since you met Jesus. What's different? How are you different?

4. If you've been a Christian for a long time (you define "long"), why do you still follow Jesus? How do you maintain a *relationship* with Him as opposed to just believing a bunch of Christian dogma because it's your "religion"?

Think this through and, as expressed in 1 Peter 3:15, stay prepared. You will be a witness for Jesus in *your* Jerusalem, *your* Judea, *your* Samaria, and to whatever end of the earth you may travel. You might also find yourself called by God to a unique ministry in a unique manner, just as I and many others have been.

He might even use garlic.

A Fresh Revelation of Jesus

Before we introduce the manual for starting and developing an effective Community Action Team (CAT) in your home area, I want to leave you with a word of encouragement. In order to do that, I need to tell you another tough-to-believe story.

It was late November 2023. I was preparing for a day-long retreat with our Restore Minnesota staff and a couple other key leaders when I sensed what the theme was to be: "A Fresh Revelation of Jesus". Now, *please*, don't let the word "revelation" throw you. Feel free to substitute it with "illumination," "picture," "understanding," or "connection". The word in my mind was "revelation" but the synonyms work just as well.

The idea of a "fresh revelation of Jesus" was exciting for all of us. It set an expectation for the day. I couldn't wait to find out what God meant by that. And then, reality hit.

The day arrived. We were going to be together from 9 a.m.-8 p.m. including a light lunch and a wonderful dinner at a nearby restaurant. We began with 30-minutes of prayer, praise, and worship. Then we sat down to get to work.

The basic instructions for the day were to have a no-holds-barred discussion on a number of issues: What are we doing well? Where are we weak? Where and what do we see the Lord doing in our CATs and communities? What did they need more of from me? Less of? From each other? What future staff do we need? Where do we sense the Lord leading us in the new year?

One of our CAT leaders asked an important question and we were off. As the day progressed, the discussions remained rich and lively. There were lots of ideas and creativity. There was thankfulness for many good things and some frustrations over other things. We worked hard, and by dinner time, we were ready to wrap it up and eat. It had been a great day together with our small and amazing team of people. We felt blessed.

Except for one thing.

As I reviewed the day upon arriving home, I was struck by the fact that in the middle of all that was good that day, we never once addressed the "fresh revelation of Jesus". I was mildly depressed because I now questioned whether or not I had blown it. How could we have missed the theme of the day?

I stewed over that for a few days, but my full schedule kept me too busy to be stuck on it. With a business conference coming up and the opening of what was expected to be a very contentious legislative session just around the corner, I had to focus on where we were going, not what we had missed. Or so I thought.

God had other plans.

Funding a ministry such as ours is not always an easy thing to do. Everyone on staff raises support, just like traditional missionaries, and we all develop other streams of income to cover both personal and ministry expenses. My wife and I run an e-commerce business and January is the time for our associates to gather in Minnesota. Fast forward from our staff retreat on December 29, 2023 to January 19–21, 2024. God showed up and He really got my attention.

There were about 1000 independent e-commerce business owners attending our conference that weekend. On opening night, while most of the attendees enjoyed an evening of games and socializing, a small group of us voluntarily gathered together to discuss important leadership issues for the weekend. For us, those issues were grounded in solid spiritual principles. It was during this time that I discovered how unusual the weekend was going to be for me.

Have you ever dislocated a rib?

There were about 45 of us in the room. Seats were arranged classroom style with a center aisle. I was seated almost directly in front of the leader of the meeting, to his right, on the aisle, second row from the front. I was simply enjoying some pre-meeting banter with my wife, who sat to my left, and with our friends in the row in front of us. In the middle of the conversation, one of my lower right ribs popped out of place.

It's hard to describe the discomfort of an out-of-place rib but, being the brave, macho male that I am, I grinned my way through it until I was able to grit my teeth and slide it back into place. Nobody knew what had happened.

That's when my lower left rib dislocated.

As I was adjusting that one, the right ribs started popping out of place. Every time I moved to adjust the side where ribs were out, the other side would start popping out. It was extremely uncomfortable. By then my wife had noticed my painful gyrations.

I am married to a wonderful woman. She has blessed me with four amazing children and stuck with me for over 50 years as of this writing. She is a sweet, gentle spirit, and when she saw me trying to push all my ribs back in place, she expressed her sincere concern. However, what I *heard* coming from my sweet, loving spouse was, "*What is wrong with you?!*" Her voice was a mixture of concern blended with mild fits of laughter.

The rib displacements lasted for *two hours.*

I struggled through that meeting, adjusting ribs until it ended. When the meeting ended, we got up to go to our hotel room and ... there were no more displaced ribs. It all stopped as suddenly as it started.

Thankfully, Saturday turned out to be predictably normal, a day of business activity just as it was planned to be. Sunday was anything but normal.

Sunday began with our traditional non-denominational worship service. Being a musician and former worship leader added to my experience in worship and it was here that I had another unusual encounter.

Have you ever been waist deep in the ocean? The current can cause you to sway rhythmically as you enjoy the movement of the tide. Sometimes it is rough enough to knock you off balance. That is exactly what happened to me that Sunday morning.

I had heard about people experiencing "waves" of the Holy Spirit, and the same was happening to me. I was being involuntarily knocked around hard enough that I had to grab the back of the chair in front of me to keep from falling down. Eventually, all I could do was fall to my knees.

When the worship time was over, we had a short break before wrapping up with our last business session. I felt an inner, ongoing buzz throughout that final session—a palpable, warm afterglow lingering from the time of praise and worship.

The weekend event ended about 3 p.m. and we headed to one of our favorite restaurants in the area. Following dinner, we drove a couple of hours to the home of our business leaders. We wanted to end it the way we started it Friday night, with scripture, prayer and worship. The group that gathered was essentially the same group that had met on Friday night. It is important to mention again that the Friday night and Sunday night gatherings, as well as the Sunday morning worship service, are not only voluntary but desired by certain members of the team. However, they are not an official part of the business meetings and certainly not mandatory. The gatherings were an opportunity for team members from around the country who don't see each other often to get together and celebrate the special bond we share as followers of Jesus who also happen to be entrepreneurs.

We met in the home's very large lower family room, packed in like sardines. The atmosphere was comfortable and the teaching challenging. I was standing behind an oversized sectional with my back against a decorative buffet table along the wall. And then it began happening again.

My ribs began popping out as they had on Friday night. But this was crazier. Much crazier.

Not only were my ribs popping out of place, but my shoulders and neck were dislocating as well, all at once. And it was *loud*. I thought everyone in the room could hear it, but that was just my imagination. To me it was as if there was a large batch of popcorn popping, and I was the popcorn! Thankfully, no one else knew what was going on.

We would soon be moving from praise and worship into a time of special personal prayer. I knew I was going to go forward for prayer. At that moment the Lord impressed upon me to be the first man in the prayer line. As I said above, we were packed in like sardines. I made my way to the prayer line as quickly as I could, only to find myself fifth in line.

But I was the first man.

Our prayer leader had us approach him one by one. I paid close attention as I listened to his prayers of deliverance for each of the four women in front of me. Even though I was experiencing these most unusual bone displacements, intuitively I knew that I did not need a prayer for deliverance. I knew that if he prayed a deliverance prayer over me, then one or both of us had missed it, whatever "it" was.

Then it was my turn.

I had known this leader for nearly 20 years, and one of the things I appreciated most about him was that he didn't rush his prayers for others. He paused long enough to hear from the Lord before praying. I waited patiently with my eyes closed, quietly praying in the Spirit, not knowing what to expect.

And then, he reached out and put his hand on my chest, over my heart. When he did so, he said, "Restore. Repair. Recreate." Then he paused a moment, his hand still over my heart, and repeated, "Restore. Repair. Recreate."

My body completely relaxed and I leaned back to lay down on the carpet.

I laid down in a very relaxed and conscious state for two minutes. Then I got up and returned to my original spot in the room between the sectional and the decorative table. I experienced that same overwhelming feeling of being driven to my knees that I had earlier at the worship service. The problem, however, was there was not enough room for me to get on my knees where I was standing, so I worked my way over to the adjacent room and slipped into the back by myself, nearly out of sight. I got down on my knees to continue in worship and found myself nearly driven face down on the carpet. I remained there for about 15 minutes.

During this time I was thinking about the words that had been spoken to me, "Restore. Repair. Recreate." I'm sure I didn't grasp the full meaning at the time, but it was while I was mulling these words over in my mind that the Lord impressed upon me that our ministry was about to go through another season of growth and expansion. He has done this a couple other times and each time new growth followed.

It was now time to leave, but the unusual encounters continued.

Remember the impression I had to be the first man in line? I didn't think any more about it until one of our young, sharp, twenty-something emerging leaders came up to me and said, "Thank you for being the first man to go forward for prayer. A lot of us younger guys felt like that gave us permission to do so as well."

Wow! Thank you, Lord! Confirmation #1!

As we began our hour-long drive home, my wife and I discussed the weekend's events in detail. Neither of us knew what to make of my experiences, but we thanked God together for what our young leader told me and for the expectation of what God was about to do in our ministry.

Confirmation #2 occurred when we arrived home. In the mail was a significant check from one of our most faithful monthly ministry supporters. It was a "first fruits" check because God was abundantly blessing their business. This particular couple is especially interested in ministries that grow and expand, so to my wife and me, the confirmation of what the Lord told me earlier in the evening was obvious.

As I climbed into bed, I couldn't help but pray prayers of thanks and expectation. I quickly fell asleep, and two more unusual things happened. First, I slept through the night. Suffice it to say that is definitely *not* normal for me. Next, and even more remarkable, is that when I woke up in the morning, my lips were still moving in prayer. Now, please understand, I have been a follower of Jesus for a *long* time and *never* in my life have I ever fallen asleep praying, slept through the night, and woke up still praying!

I was immediately conscious of this, and that is when the Lord spoke clearly to me.

I want you, the reader, to know that I have recounted this very extraordinary series of events just to get to this point in the story. Everything I've said in this final chapter of the book is to tell you what I'm about to tell you.

The Lord awakened me with the following message:

"Of all of the choices you will make today, choose Me. Consecrate yourselves for I am about to revive and restore Minnesota."

Please read those two sentences again.

Differing sources agree that the average person makes about 35,000 decisions *every day*! Think about it. You and I will make all kinds of decisions today, conscious and subconscious. Getting out of bed is a decision. Making that first cup of coffee is a decision. Driving down the road and turning right, turning left, or going straight is a decision. To finish reading this book is a decision. All of us, every day, make about *35,000* decisions.

The Lord is asking us to make one very conscious, very intentional daily decision. The decision is: Choose Him. In all of our 35,000 decisions today, the most important one is to choose Him. How do we do that?

We consecrate ourselves. That means we make a conscious choice each day to dedicate ourselves, devote ourselves, and set ourselves apart for God's purposes and desires.

When the Lord spoke this to me, I immediately thought of Joshua 3:5.

Joshua was Moses' right hand man. When Moses climbed his last mountain and passed into glory, Joshua became the leader of the Hebrew people. As Joshua prepared to lead the people into the land God had promised them, he went off alone to pray. During that time in prayer, Joshua had a face-to-face meeting with Jesus Himself, the Commander of the Lord's Army. The result of that meeting led Joshua to pull all of the Hebrew people together and tell them, "Consecrate yourselves, for tomorrow the Lord will do wonders among you."

The Lord is instructing us to consecrate ourselves, for He is about to revive and restore Minnesota. Many of you reading this are thinking, "But, I am not in Minnesota." I get it. Please, hang in here with me.

There have been many prayers and prophetic words over the state of Minnesota. Indeed, Minnesota is known as the revival state. Minnesota is to play a significant role in the next major national revival. How is God going to do this? I do not know. *When* is God going to do this? I do not know. But I believe He will.

There are many reasons why, and here is one of them:

I was given a copy of a picture years ago by a former state legislator during our weekly legislative Bible study. He told me the story of a picture showing a fireball of revival hitting a state capitol building somewhere in the United States, but he couldn't verify the details to know whether or not the story was true. He told me from whom he had received it. I called that person, and she couldn't remember who gave it to her. I was at a dead end.

The verification was given to me by the leader of our statewide intercessory prayer network at a national security conference a few months later. I had no idea she was going to attend, due to the secure vetting process for the event. When I saw her there, I approached her and asked if she knew anything about the picture. I showed it to her. She nonchalantly let me know that she was the one who had received it from Honduras and made it public!

Several months later I purchased a book by Dale Gilmore, *Minnesota: The Revival State—Moves of God 1860– 1960*, and read the following:

> A Youth With A Mission (YWAM) pastor from Honduras who knows nothing about the capitol buildings in each of our states, had a vision from the Lord over a decade ago.
>
> Here's the actual story, copied from pages 435 and 436 of the book:
>
> On January 30, 2015, a group of about 200 Spirit-filled young adults from Central America, South America, and the United States were worshiping the Lord at an intensive prophetic training conference in Honduras. During worship, a young man from Honduras named Sergio received a vision of a type of 'capitol building' in the United States. He 'saw' a 'fireball' coming toward the top of this government building, though the 'fireball' had not yet hit the building. At the top of the building was a large dome with a 'gold' object at the peak of the dome and 'gold' statues near the base of the dome. The

young man, Sergio, described the 'fireball' as the 'fire of God'.

Sergio and his wife, Melissa, run a Youth With a Mission base in Honduras. As he described the vision to his wife, she thought the building could be the US Capitol. She used her phone to find a picture of the US Capitol building, but he said that it was not the building that he saw in the vision. As Sergio described the building further to his wife who is from Minnesota, she thought the building sounded like the Minnesota State Capitol. She pulled up a picture of this building on her phone and Sergio said that the Minnesota State Capitol building was the government building in his vision. Sergio has never visited Minnesota. Sergio then used his artistic ability to draw the vision in a sketchbook while referring to the picture of the Minnesota State Capitol Building on his wife Melissa's phone.

In addition, my friend, Karen Krueger, and another friend, Linda Holmes, who helped edit the book, are referenced within for their contributions. Karen is the leader of our intercessory prayer network and verified the picture for me at the national security conference I mentioned above!

Here is the picture:

While there are several implications to all of this remember the following:

1. When Jesus said from the cross, "It is finished," victory over sin and death was declared.
2. When Jesus was resurrected from the grave, victory over sin and death and the offer of a new quality of life to all who will believe was confirmed.
3. When the scriptures tell us in the very final book of the Bible, the Book of Revelation, that Jesus is King and He reigns, that is a current reality, not just a future promise.

As followers of Jesus Christ, it is imperative we remember that we are not fighting today's battles hoping *for* victory. We are fighting today's battles *from* victory. We are like an occupying army whose job is to continue to clean out the pockets of resistance from a defeated enemy. We do that family by family, community by community, and county by county. We do so knowing we have already won and that to God belongs all the credit and glory!

So, as we wrap up the story portion of *Courageous Christianity* and before we move on to the practical application section "Walking It Out," please dwell in prayer over these words from the Lord:

"Of all of the choices you will make today, choose Me. Consecrate yourselves for I am about to revive and restore Minnesota."

Let it be, Lord Jesus! Amen and amen.

Epilogue

An epilogue is not normally necessary, but in this case I believe it is. Today is Tuesday, July 23, 2024. It was just ten days ago that the enemy of our souls tried to interrupt God's plans with the assassination attempt of presidential candidate Donald J. Trump. I am not writing this to be political. I am not writing this to demonstrate support for any particular candidate. I am trying to state what to me is obvious: the enemy of our souls hates the United States of America. He hates our Constitution. He hates our Declaration of Independence. He hates American values and ideals, and he will do anything to cause chaos in our culture. This chaos is being intensified with the apparent coup the Democrat Party successfully conducted by "convincing" the current President, Joe Biden, the one who received over 14 million votes from his party to be the Presidential candidate for 2024, to drop out of the race.

Why does satan hate America so much?

Because the contents and principles in our founding documents are based primarily on the Bible, the Word of God.

The Bible has a lot to say about Biblical citizenship and the role of the church in the arena of government, as well as every arena of society. But, we have become ignorant of both our Biblical founding and the role of pastors in that founding. We have been fed lies for decades so that current generations believe as truth that which is really untrue. It is time for a Great Awakening in our land. Great Awakenings are God-driven and God-led. But, while we wait on God and His perfect timing, it is our responsibility to wake up and take God-directed action.

You have just read the story of how God initiated and continues to lead a ministry committed to restoring righteousness in America. Like Nehemiah's wall, it begins in each of our own backyards. As you move into the *Walking It Out* portion of this book, ask God what he wants done in your home, your community, your county, and your state. Ask Him what your part is to be in the development of a Community Action Team (CAT) or our new initiative, the *Institute for Biblical Citizenship*. Once He answers, Restore Minnesota stands ready to assist you in creating Restore (Name Your State). You can reach us at www.RestoreMN.org or at PO Box 282, Saint Michael, MN 55376.

Let's lock arms across America. We've got a nation to save!

Walking It Out:
A Manual for
Restoring Righteousness in
America through *Community*
Action Teams (CATs)

This manual contains a nuts-and-bolts approach to starting and establishing a Community Action Team wherever you live as a strategic activation of the Purpose and Mission of the Restore Minnesota ministry. It is intended as a recommended sequence for the first 10 meetings of a new CAT. Every startup will be different, but all the suggestions in this manual have been used at some point in the creation of CATs across Minnesota.

I hope this manual will provide guidelines as you begin the process or offer suggestions for group exercises for existing CAT leaders to further establish and grow their teams.

Dan Montague, Senior Steward, Restore Minnesota

PRE-LAUNCH

After initial interest in a community has been established, usually through an in-person or online gathering of like-minded Christians and Patriots, it is time to plan a Kickoff Meeting. A meeting date and place must be secured. It is important to extend personal invitations to those within the initial group's sphere of influence. We strongly recommend that all invitations to a CAT be personal, especially in the early stages. We recommend not using public invitations or social media. We also recommend that media not attend—these are private meetings.

Following is a general outline of an agenda for the Kickoff Meeting. Please see Supplement #1 for a suggested agenda for on-going regular meetings. RMN (Restore Minnesota) Staff will usually commit to being at the first three meetings, if possible. Efforts must be made to identify a Team Leader/Facilitator or potential members of a Leadership Council (see Supplement #4) as soon as possible.

[Note: Most of our existing CATs started with an individual or couple as the Team Leader(s). That is the easiest way to get things going. However, in many cases it has become necessary to have a Leadership Council share the responsibilities. This is due to both the time commitment and physical effort required of leaders, as well as the spiritual opposition that many encounter. There is strength and encouragement in having a leadership team.]

KICKOFF MEETING (Facilitated by RMN Staff)

Goals: Get acquainted — Overview of Restore Minnesota — Explanation of a Community Action Team.

1. Introductions (everyone):
   a. Name
   b. What community do you live in?
   c. Who invited you? Or, how did you hear about this meeting?
   d. Why did you come?
2. What is Restore Minnesota? (with handouts)
   a. Foundational positions
   b. God honoring
   c. Christ centered
   d. Bible based
   e. Holy Spirit-led
   f. Five Pillars
3. What is a Community Action Team?
   a. General description
   b. Introduce the idea of Task Forces
   c. Encourage the "pray-ers" to consider becoming part of the Intercessors Task Force
4. How does Restore Minnesota with CATs relate to the 7 Mission Fields (Mountains) of Cultural Influence?
   a. Three Institutions created by God
      i. Family
      ii. Government
      iii. Church
   b. Success stories of active CATs
5. Everyone invite another person to the next meeting.

MEETING #2 (Full Group Discussion — Facilitated by RMN Staff)

Goal: Establish an overview of issues and concerns in this county/community.

Note: For this discussion, an issue is a concern that was not dealt with in a timely manner and now has a real or potential negative impact to the community.

1. Ask for everyone's participation to brainstorm about what is happening, or not happening, in this community/county that is an issue or a concern.
   a. Rules:
      i. Every idea matters
      ii. Stay respectful, no criticism allowed
      iii. One person at a time
      iv. Purpose is to generate ideas, not defend them
   b. Try to stay with local issues and concerns, although state and federal actions do affect the local community, e.g. election integrity, federal mandates, etc.
2. Ideas will be written on a white board or flip chart.
3. Everyone invite another person to the next meeting.
4. If possible, establish and appoint a local team leader/facilitator for this CAT or move toward the creation of a Leadership Council who will share the responsibilities of leading the CAT meetings.

MEETING #3 (Small Group Discussions — Facilitated by New CAT Leader/Facilitator and RMN Staff)
Goal: At least two small groups will continue the brainstorming process, expanding on the previous week's ideas and starting to offer possible solutions.

1. A decision will be made by RMN Staff prior to the meeting as to which general areas the small groups will focus (usually corresponding to the 7 Mountains or Mission Fields of Cultural Influence). Note: the two most common general areas tend to be Education and Government (especially election integrity).

2. A handout will be provided outlining the brainstorming ideas from Meeting #2.

3. Each small group must have a leader and a scribe to take notes.

4. Everyone is encouraged to share in their small groups, following the same brainstorming rules as before.

5. Allow time at the close of the meeting for small group reports from the leader or scribe. Note: Each group's notes must be provided to the CAT Facilitator and RMN Staff.

6. Everyone invite another person to the next meeting.

MEETING #4 (Small Group Discussions — This meeting, and all meetings going forward, will be facilitated by a newly appointed CAT Facilitator or someone from the newly formed Leadership Council)
Goal: The same small groups will move the brainstorming process toward more clearly identifying and prioritizing issues

and concerns, while discussing needed solutions and possible corresponding actions.

1. A handout will be provided outlining the brainstorming ideas of Meeting #3.
2. Each small group must have a leader and a scribe (to take notes).
3. Everyone is encouraged to share in their small groups, following the same brainstorming rules as before.
4. Three primary questions for each group to discuss are:
   a. What has been done in the community/ county to address the issues/concerns being identified and prioritized?
   b. Who—individual, group, or organization—is doing something?
   c. What could be done going forward, either to support what is happening or to start a new effort?
5. Allow time at the close of the meeting for small group reports from the leader or scribe. Note: Each group's notes must be provided to the CAT Facilitator.
6. Everyone invite another person for next week.

MEETING #5 (Exercise in Critical Thinking)
Goal: Allow for an appropriate number of small groups (probably two or three) who will step back from brainstorming and evaluate their own thought processes regarding the issues and concerns discussed in previous weeks. That is, to review what they have been thinking about and ask themselves "Why?"

The focus will be on paradigms that have changed in recent years.

1. The CAT Meeting Facilitator will do a brief presentation/explanation about paradigms including examples (notes provided in Supplement #2).

2. Each small group must have a leader to guide the discussion, but no scribe. Individuals sharing will be optional at the end of the meeting.

3. Everyone is encouraged to share, with the trust and confidence built over the past meetings that they will be heard and respected in their small groups.

4. The guiding questions for each small group member are:

    a. What paradigm(s) have I believed about government/education/medical/ church/etc. that have changed in recent years?

    b. Once identified, the follow-up questions are: when and why did the paradigm(s) change.

5. Allow time at the close of the meeting for a few individuals to share with the whole group.

6. Everyone invite another person for next week.

MEETING #6 (Guest speaker)
Goal: Begin to educate and equip the group through a presentation by an outside expert in one of the primary areas of concern—topics could be Critical Race Theory, Comprehensive Sex Education, the function of School Boards, Sex Trafficking, Law Enforcement, Medical Freedom, Election Integrity, the Role of Christians in Government, etc. RMN Staff and the

CAT Facilitator will work together to secure a speaker for this meeting immediately following Meeting #2.

1. Allow plenty of time for the speaker and Q&A. Suggestion: Have a couple of people pray for the guest speaker at the end and for God's blessings of wisdom, revelation, health, protection, and provision.

2. Prep the group beforehand that a free-will offering will be taken for the speaker. Have a basket or bucket set out. Get instructions from RMN staff on handling the money.

3. Everyone invite another person for next week.

MEETING #7 (Introduction of Task Forces)
Goal: Move the small discussion groups toward a task force model.

1. Review, recap, and provide highlights of previous week's guest speaker presentation. Get feedback from the whole group.

2. CAT Meeting Facilitator will lead a short group teaching/discussion defining a Task Force.

   a. Brief overview of all the listed task forces in Supplement #3

   b. Allow a little time for any additional task force suggestions

      i. Handouts: definition of a task force along with the descriptions of the task forces being implemented, usually starting with Intercessors, Grass Roots (Local) Government, and Education (or others based on the interests of the group).

  ii. Task force leaders will be introduced. (Determined by the CAT Facilitator prior to this meeting, often resulting from observation of leadership skills exhibited in the small group discussions of previous weeks. They may volunteer or need to be asked.)

  iii. Allow for most of the time to be given to the new task forces.

  iv. They will start working on the specifics of their primary purposes as described.

  v. Those leaning toward Intercessors can spend the time praying

  vi. Explain that going forward, there will normally be time allotted in the regular CAT meetings for task forces to meet.

3. Everyone invite another person for next week.

MEETING #8 (Task Forces)

Goal: Expand the task force concept and encourage greater participation.

1. CAT Meeting Facilitator will review what a Task Force is and which ones are being formed in this Community Action Team.

 a. Focus on those Task Forces from Supplement #3 (or others) that were started last week

 b. Handouts: definition of a task force along with the descriptions of the task forces being implemented

 c. Task force leaders will be acknowledged/ introduced

d. Allow most of the time to be given to the new task forces

e. They will continue working on the specifics of their primary purposes as described

f. Those leaning toward Intercessors can spend the time praying

g. Remind the whole group that going forward, there will normally be time allotted in the regular CAT meetings for task forces to meet.

2. Everyone invite another person for next week.

MEETING #9 (Full Group Discussion)

Goal: Sharing of information on local current events that are impacting the county/community/families.

1. The CAT Meeting Facilitator will lead an open discussion of the full group on a pressing current event (e.g., loss of jobs in the area due to vaccine mandates, actions of the local school board, proposed zoning changes by the city council, etc.) to educate the group and increase awareness of that topic. Allow members to respond with personal experience, information, and encouragement for the group. This exercise will easily shift to other relevant topics. The Facilitator is encouraged to allow some leeway in the group discussion while maintaining order.

a. While this may offer some challenges to the Facilitator, it can be a rewarding group experience

b. This full group discussion is expected to go smoothly, building on the respect, trust, and confidence exhibited in the small groups and task forces over the past meetings

2. These "open discussion" CAT meetings often become a favorite of those who attend.

3. Everyone invite another person for next week.

MEETING #10 (Guest speaker)

Goal: Continue to educate and equip the group through a presentation by an outside expert in one of the primary areas of concern. Topics could be Critical Race Theory, Comprehensive Sex Education, the function of School Boards, Sex Trafficking, Law Enforcement, Medical Freedom, Election Integrity, the role of Christians in Government, etc. RMN Staff and the CAT Facilitator will work together to secure a speaker immediately following Meeting #6

1. Allow plenty of time for the speaker and Q&A. Suggestion: have a couple of people pray for the guest speaker at the end and for God's blessings of wisdom, revelation, health, protection, and provision.

2. Prep the group beforehand that a free-will offering will be taken for the speaker. Have a basket or bucket set out. Get instructions from RMN staff on handling the money.

3. Everyone invite another person for next week.

Going Forward:

1. Regularly allot time in the CAT meetings for Task Forces to meet together to plan their goals,

strategies, and activities, (i.e., a Task Force Breakout Session).

2. Regularly schedule outside guest speakers—once each month works well. Recommended lists of speakers/topics are being compiled by RMN Staff.

3. Individuals within the CAT may have an area of expertise they could speak about that would be good to share with the full group when appropriate.

4. We suggest starting with regular *weekly* CAT meetings, if possible, to build depth and momentum in the group. It is important to help those attending get answers to the questions, "What are the issues/concerns in my community?" and then, "What can we do about it?" This happens through the process of educating, equipping, and empowering, and leads to encouraging ourselves and each other in Holy Spirit-led engagement. At that point, some CATs go to fewer group meetings each month (twice a month is common) so that CAT members can do more with Task Forces, attend School Board meetings, attend County Board and City Council meetings, assist righteous candidates at various levels of local and state government, etc.

5. Be quick to reach out to RMN staff for assistance with any questions, concerns, or issues. Be assured, they will arise! RMN's concern is not CATs asking for help too much—it is not asking often enough!

Supplement #1
Suggested CAT Meeting Agenda

1. Registration table (area) for sign in and name tags

2. Welcome (start on time):
    a. Opening Prayer
    b. Pledge of Allegiance (you may consider trying the pledge at the end of the meeting)
    c. Phones off and any facility rules such as no food, water only, etc.
    d. Introduction of first-time guests: names, where from, who invited, why did they come, etc.
    e. Overview of the night's focus: task force work session, guest speaker, etc.
    f. Preview of the next week's meeting: task forces, speaker, etc.

3. Restore Minnesota Purpose and Mission (occasionally review the Vision/Strategy/Values/Framework)

4. Devotional (keep to 3–5 minutes)

5. Announcements/Upcoming (most announcements should be handled through an email calendar/ updates):
    a. New events that did not get into the email calendar
    b. Events that need to be highlighted for CAT action or involvement
    c. Other

6. Reports (goal of no more than three minutes per report):
   a. Task forces: if the meeting is devoted to task force work sessions, you may reserve a few minutes at the end for their reports
   b. Other important government board meetings attended
   c. Important local events that happened, especially if attended by a CAT member
   d. Other

7. Program:
   a. Break into groups/task forces … or
   b. Introduce guest speaker (allow 60 minutes for presentation including Q&A) … or
   c. Other planned program

8. Close/Prayer
   a. Emphasize any facility rules about chairs, cleanup, etc.

Supplement #2
Paradigms

A *paradigm* is a way of thinking about an issue or topic. Our combined paradigms will determine how we reflect on life in general. Paradigms become a framework of our belief system, the thought filters through which we perceive and then process information. Some synonyms are: frame of mind, mindset, belief, filter, lens.

An example of a paradigm about education is: Public Schools always look out for the best interests of our children. Another is: We can trust teachers to properly educate our children.

An example of a paradigm about government is: Our federal or state government truly cares about the health and safety of the citizens.

Supplement #3
Community Action Team Task Forces

Task Force: a subgroup of the Community Action Team consisting of two or more people focusing on an area of community concern that comes out of the full CAT group discussion or from CAT leadership. They are charged with the development of ideas, strategies, and action items to help mobilize the Community Action Team to interact, influence, and impact the community in that area of concern. They must meet regularly and report to CAT leadership and the full group consistently, except for the Intercessors Task Force due to the more private aspects of their function.

Following are suggested task forces and their purposes currently being utilized or considered by active CATs. Others may develop going forward.

Intercessors (A necessary task force)

Primary purposes:

    A. Cover the local CAT meetings, activities, and leadership with prayer.

    B. Ask God for divine wisdom and revelation to bring about the Restore Minnesota objective: "Holy Spirit-led prayer releases God-directed action."

    C. Decree and declare that we have authority over the enemy (satan) and that none of his schemes or strategies will hinder the God-directed actions of the Community Action Team as a whole, including CAT weekly meetings, CAT Task Forces, CAT leadership, or the individual team members.

    D. Whenever possible, CAT leadership and Task Force leaders will direct specific prayer needs or concerns to the Intercessors Task Force and provide updates and answers (praise reports) as they occur.

    E. This Intercessors Task Force will also pray over all the MN CATs in operation, for CATs in the process of forming or yet to be formed, and the overall operation, leadership, and financial support of Restore Minnesota.

    F. Pray as led by the Holy Spirit regarding concerns and issues in the communities represented by the local CAT.

    G. And more …

Grassroots (Local) Government Task Force (A common task force)

Primary purposes:

A. Identify all the local governing bodies in the CAT area. Who are the present elected officials, when do their current terms end, when and where do they meet, and what are the concerns and issues they are dealing with (or *should be* dealing with)?

B. Also identify the ad hoc committees and task forces that operate under the various boards and governing bodies mentioned above.

C. Encourage and assist in mobilizing the full CAT membership to attend the various board meetings consistently and to coordinate any opportunities to speak at these meetings regarding specific issues.

D. Identify, offer support, and pray for local government candidates who have courage and moral fortitude while standing for Godly, conservative principles, who will prioritize the rights of "we the people".

E. Plan, write, and send strategic letters to the editor identifying issues of concern in the CAT area, and rebut letters others have sent.

F. Explore opportunities to serve the various local/ county governing bodies.

This task force will become the "watchmen on the wall" regarding anything these local elected officials present, propose, or pass that is ungodly, unnecessary, unhealthy, or unfunded (not in the budget).

Election Integrity (May function separately or as component of the Local Government Task Force)
Primary purposes:

A. Discover the main issues of election irregularities in the CAT area.

B. Identify other groups and organizations already working to uncover and correct these election issues, and work with them toward a common goal as much as possible.

C. Identify the local governing bodies (elected and non-elected) that control any part of the election process (e.g., the voting machines are set in place by the County Commissioner Board).

D. Encourage and assist in mobilizing the full CAT membership to attend appropriate board meetings (e.g., County Commissioners) consistently and to coordinate any opportunities to speak at these meetings regarding election integrity issues.

E. Plan, write, and send strategic letters to the editor regarding these election issues in the CAT area, and rebut letters others have sent.

F. Explore opportunities to serve any other group or local/county governing or political bodies that are cooperating with the goal of full election integrity (e.g., helping to clean up voter rolls, digital and physical canvassing).

G. Educate and encourage the full CAT membership about getting involved in the final voting process: election judges, poll watchers, ballot boards, etc.

H. And more ...

Education (A common task force)

Primary purposes:

A. Identify the public school districts in the CAT area.

B. Discover existing groups of parents or concerned citizens that are monitoring and engaging area public school boards and school administrations. Offer support as appropriate.

C. Identify the present school board members in each district, when their current terms end, and when and where they meet. Learn what concerns and issues they are dealing with, or *should be* dealing with, such as Critical Race Theory, Comprehensive Sex Education, and pornographic books in the library or even in the curriculum. Also identify the ad hoc committees and task forces that operate under the school boards (e.g., curriculum).

D. Encourage and assist in mobilizing the full CAT membership to attend the school board meetings consistently and to coordinate any opportunities to speak at these meetings regarding specific issues.

E. Identify, offer support, and pray for school board candidates who have courage and moral fortitude while standing for Godly, conservative principles and who will prioritize parents' rights and concerns.

F. Plan, write, and send strategic letters to the editor identifying critical issues in the school district, and rebut letters others have sent.

G. Explore opportunities to serve the local/county school boards and administrations.

This task force will become the "watchmen on the wall" regarding anything the local school boards or administrations present, propose, or pass that is ungodly, unnecessary, unhealthy, or unfunded (not in the budget).

In addition, this task force will discover and gather information on public school alternatives in the community/county (e.g., charter schools, private schools, homeschool co-ops, micro schools, etc.).

Community Logistics (aka Creative Community Life) (A developing task force)

Primary purposes: Discover skills, assets, and resources within the CAT membership that might become important to manage and share if economic, governmental, or environmental conditions (natural disasters) bring about shortages of utilities, food, transportation, etc. Identify common neighborhoods of CAT members to better coordinate and help each other. Strategize ways to assist other neighbors who may experience fearful or desperate situations. Bring awareness that preparing for possible difficult times includes not only the physical aspects, but also spiritual, emotional, mental, financial, relational, and more. Seek strategies from God that will help CAT members not only survive but thrive as we strive to impact the greater community for the Gospel of Jesus Christ

Additional: Community Logistics Mission and Objectives

Mission – To be an instrument of Restore MN by assisting our members and communities in developing Christ-centered resiliency skills to be prepared for normal life and any event considered a disruption of "normal life."

Objectives – The following steps are still being developed:

1. Establish a main core team to compile and create documentation.
2. Identify individuals with major areas of expertise and invite them to contribute.
3. Establish small teams, referred to as PODs, formed according to proximity (walking distance).
4. Provide education & encouragement, enabling members to stand strong and serve well.

Community is defined as a group of people unified around a common purpose, interest, or characteristic or the physical location in which a group of people resides. Our Restore MN Teams are indeed a **community** by both definitions.

Logistics can refer to the coordination of people regarding accomplishing group goals, or the overall process of managing resources available to a group. Both meanings apply to our activities as we move forward— serving each other, honoring the Lord, and making the world a better place by expanding His dominion.

Our purpose is to prepare materials that encourage Restore MN members to **learn** practical skills, equipping them to **grow** in resiliency and resourceful living in every area, so each of us may be able to **serve** enthusiastically in preserving faith, life, liberty, and community, as protected under the United States Constitution.

Standing with the Lord, we believe we are tougher than any difficulty which may present itself and that powerful lessons are learned in challenging times. We expect not only to survive but thrive and emerge a stronger, more faith-filled people as a result of these adventures.

As we undertake this quest of **learning, growing, and serving together,** we acknowledge that we are just normal people who love our families, friends, and communities. Our efforts to prepare are born from this deep love, and we realize we are not prepared unless our neighbor is also prepared. It takes a resilient, faithful community to thrive.

Therefore, we are doing everything we realistically can to grow ourselves and prepare our families along with others (YOU!) for an unknown and challenging future ahead. We don't fear what the future may bring. We love life, the Lord, and each other as we move into that future with faith and gratitude for all God has blessed us with. We invite you to join us in trusting God and expecting His blessing as together, we face whatever the future brings by living a self-reliant, faith-filled, resilient, and productive lifestyle.

Non-Governmental Organizations (NGOs) (An increasingly important task force)

Primary purpose:

A. Discover and then increase the full CAT awareness of the NGOs operating in the CAT area through research and bringing in guest expert speakers. These NGOs may include Sourcewell or one of its affiliates, the League of Cities, Regional Planners in Regional Development Boards, refugee resettlement initiatives, and major grants with significant strings attached from McKnight, Blandin, Bush, and others.

B. Warn local governing bodies of the Marxist agendas of these NGOs, including U.N. Agenda 2030, Green Steps, etc.

C. Bring public exposure of the true intent of these NGOs as appropriate.

Other Potential Task Forces

- **Medical Freedom**
- **Church and Pastor Relations**
- **Community Service Projects**
- **Other**

Supplement #4
Suggestions for forming a CAT Leadership Council (CLC)

The CLC shall consist of:

- CAT Leader/Facilitator and spouse (if involved in the CAT and interested)
- Leaders of active task forces and spouses (if involved in the CAT and interested), who will serve in the CLC through the duration of their leadership of a task force
- At least one, but no more than two, at-large CAT members, at the invitation of the CAT Leader or RMN Staff, who agree to serve on the CLC for a period of at least twelve months

Purpose

The general purpose of this group is to be an advisory/executive board to the CAT Leader. It will give substance to the wisdom of Proverbs that says, "plans fail for lack of counsel, but with many advisers they succeed."

The CAT Leadership Council will:

1. Explore broader considerations of the CAT as a whole, while focusing on the growth, development, and function of the CAT, including:
   a. What is working well
   b. What could we do better
   c. How do we reach more people
   d. Are we tracking with the Restore Minnesota purpose, mission, and goals

    e.   Do we have the right mix of spiritual emphasis
    f.   What topics would be good to address
    g.   Who would be a good speaker on those topics
    h.   Would a new task force on that topic be beneficial
    i.   And more

2. Offer and discuss ideas specific to the development and function of the existing task forces.
3. Provide logistical support to the CAT Leader in planning and conducting meetings, such as:
    a.   Helping to arrange for meeting hosts and room setup as needed
    b.   Helping to arrange for a meeting facilitator as needed, including taking turns leading meetings and devotions

Meetings

The CLC shall meet _(how often & when)_ at a place to be decided by the CLC. Occasionally, the CAT Leader may call for a special meeting. Other CLC communications may occur via email, private messaging, and video meetings.

Appendix

The Role of the Church in Government

Watch for a more complete discussion regarding the church's role in government in our upcoming book, *The Role of the Church in Government*. In the meantime, here is a brief summary.

- Matthew 16:18 – Jesus said he came to build His *ekklesia*. In Jesus's day, that was a political/ governmental statement, not a religious statement. (cf. Isaiah 9:6)
- 1 Tim. 2:1–4 – Christians are to pray continually for their governmental leaders, especially for their salvation. Could it be that the purpose of having governmental leaders who are saved is not only so that they can go to heaven when they die but that they might also govern in a godly manner while they are in office?
- Proverbs 29:2 – It is the job of the church to raise righteous men and women, some of whom God can use in governmental leadership. If the people are to be blessed by righteous leaders, who but

the church can raise those whom the Bible would consider to be righteous?

- Proverbs 14:34 – If "righteousness exalts a nation," who but the church can raise righteous men and women to serve in positions of servant leadership in every Mission Field of Culture?
- Proverbs 28:12 – There is great glory when righteousness wins out.
- Exodus 18:21 – America's founding fathers used this verse not only to remind us of the desired character of people put into leadership, but also as a model for creating a new governmental system as outlined in our Declaration of Independence and fleshed out in greater detail in its corresponding document, the Constitution of the United States.
- Daniel 4:27 – A great reminder to those in leadership, perhaps especially for those in government.
- Jeremiah 29:7 – God is concerned about cities and their well-being.
- Matthew 14:3–4; Luke 3:18–20 – John the Baptist is a model for the church's voice to speak into the government and hold it accountable.
- Romans 13:1–7; 1 Peter 2:13–15 – Good government protects the righteous and punishes the wicked. Government that promotes evil is evil.
- Philippians 1:27 – Do politics worthy of the gospel of Jesus Christ (classical Greek).

Pastors, Churches, and Other Roadblocks

Here are some thoughts I've been asked to address over the years:

1. **You cannot legislate morality.**

    Not true. Every bit of legislation represents somebody's morality. America was founded by men who believed that Biblical morality should be reflected in our laws.

2. **I have Democrats and Republicans in my church.**

    That is code for "I don't want somebody's check to walk out the door." Nobody is asking you to be Democrat or Republican. America's congregations are asking their pastors to be Biblical and to address crucial cultural issues from the pulpit. According to a recent report by George Barna, only 14 percent of America's pastors are willing to do so. (See the Biblical Worldview section at FRC.org). Furthermore, the check walking out your door is not the source of your financial security, no matter how big that check is. Pastors need to have more "fear of the Lord" than we have "fear of the Board". God is our Source and Provider. Remember: Jesus let the rich young ruler walk away.

3. **What about the separation of church and state?**

    What about it? It is not in the Constitution. The two entities, church and government, were separated by our founders—not to keep the church out of government but to keep the government out of the affairs of the church. Lack of separation was the normal practice in Europe. Our founders wanted nothing to do with the European model. Thomas Jefferson said, "When we get piled upon one another in large cities, as in Europe, we shall become as corrupt as Europe."

"This is a genuine quotation, although slightly altered from the original, which reads, 'I think our governments will remain virtuous for many centuries; as long as they are chiefly agricultural; and this will be as long as there shall be vacant lands in any part of America. When they get piled upon one another in large cities, as in Europe, they will become corrupt as in Europe.'" Jefferson is the man who coined the phrase "the wall of separation" in response to a concern raised by the Danbury Baptists of Danbury, Connecticut. Their concern was that a particular denomination would be named the "official" denomination of the United States, much like the Church of England. Jefferson assured them it would not happen, but he did not suggest the church and state should not work together. He approved and attended church in the nation's Capitol building and even approved the United States Marine Corp band to serve as the "worship team". When one reads the writings of the Founding Fathers, one realizes they would have been aghast at the thought of keeping the teachings of the Bible out of the government.

The 45 Goals of the Communist Party[2]

On January 10, 1963, Congressman Albert S. Herlong Jr. of Florida read a list of 45 Communist goals into the Congressional Record. The list was derived from researcher and former FBI Agent, W. Cleon Skousen's book *The Naked Communist*. These principles are well worth revisiting today to gain insights into the thinking and strategies of much of our so-called liberal elite:

1. U.S. should accept coexistence as the only alternative to atomic war.
2. U.S. should be willing to capitulate in preference to engaging in atomic war.
3. Develop the illusion that total disarmament by the U.S. would be a demonstration of "moral strength".
4. Permit free trade between all nations regardless of Communist affiliation and regardless of whether or not items could be used for war.
5. Extend long-term loans to Russia and Soviet satellites.
6. Provide American aid to all nations regardless of Communist domination.
7. Grant recognition of Red China and admission of Red China to the U.N.
8. Set up East and West Germany as separate states in spite of Khrushchev's promise in 1955 to settle

---

2   Donald Boyd, Donalds's Thoughts blog, uploaded from *The Naked Communist*, the-naked-communist-goals-with-notes-and-highlights.pdf (donaldboyd.org).

the Germany question by free elections under supervision of the U.N.

9. Prolong the conferences to ban atomic tests because the U.S. has agreed to suspend tests as long as negotiations are in progress.

10. Allow all Soviet satellites individual representation in the U.N.

11. Promote the U.N. as the only hope for mankind. If its charter is rewritten, demand that it be set up as a one-world government with its own independent armed forces.

12. Resist any attempt to outlaw the Communist Party.

13. Do away with loyalty oaths.

14. Continue giving Russia access to the U.S. Patent Office.

15. Capture one or both of the political parties in the U.S.

16. Use technical decisions of the courts to weaken basic American institutions, by claiming their activities violate civil rights.

17. Get control of the schools. Use them as transmission belts for Socialism and current Communist propaganda. Soften the curriculum. Get control of teachers associations. Put the party line in textbooks.

18. Gain control of all student newspapers.

19. Use student riots to foment public protests against programs or organizations that are under Communist attack.

20. Infiltrate the press. Get control of book review assignments, editorial writing, policy-making positions.

21. Gain control of key positions in radio, TV & motion pictures.

22. Continue discrediting American culture by degrading all forms of artistic expression. An American Communist cell was told to "eliminate all good sculpture from parks and buildings," substituting shapeless, awkward, and meaningless forms.

23. Control art critics and directors of art museums. "Our plan is to promote ugliness, repulsive, meaningless art."

24. Eliminate all laws governing obscenity by calling them "censorship" and a violation of free speech and free press.

25. Break down cultural standards of morality by promoting pornography and obscenity in books, magazines, motion pictures, radio, and TV.

26. Present homosexuality, degeneracy, and promiscuity as "normal, natural and healthy." [Note: Today those few who still have the courage to advocate public morality are denounced and viciously attacked. Most Americans are entirely unwitting regarding the motives behind this agenda.]

27. Infiltrate the churches and replace revealed religion with "social" religion. Discredit the Bible and emphasize the need for intellectual maturity, which does not need a "religious crutch."

28. Eliminate prayer or any phase of religious expression in the schools on the grounds that it violates the principle of "separation of church and state.".

29. Discredit the American Constitution by calling it inadequate, old fashioned, out of step with modern needs, a hindrance to cooperation between nations on a worldwide basis.

30. Discredit the American founding fathers. Present them as selfish aristocrats who had no concern for the "common man."

31. Belittle all forms of American culture and discourage the teaching of American history on the grounds that it was only a minor part of "the big picture." Give more emphasis to Russian history since the Communists took over.

32. Support any socialist movement to give centralized control over any part of the culture—education, social agencies, welfare programs, mental health clinics, etc.

33. Eliminate all laws or procedures which interfere with the operation of the Communist apparatus.

34. Eliminate the House Committee on Un-American Activities.

35. Discredit and eventually dismantle the FBI.

36. Infiltrate and gain control of more unions.

37. Infiltrate and gain control of big business.

38. Transfer some of the powers of arrest from the police to social agencies. Treat all behavioral problems as psychiatric disorders which no one but psychiatrists can understand or treat.

39. Dominate the psychiatric profession and use mental health laws as a means of gaining coercive control over those who oppose communist goals.

40. Discredit the family as an institution. Encourage promiscuity and easy divorce.

41. Emphasize the need to raise children away from the negative influence of parents. Attribute prejudices, mental blocks, and retarding of children to suppressive influence of parents. [Note: Outcome-based education, values clarification, or whatever they're calling it this year.]

42. Create the impression that violence and insurrection are legitimate aspects of the American tradition; that students and special interest groups should rise up and make a "united force" to solve economic, political, or social problems.

43. Overthrow all colonial governments before native populations are ready for self-government.

44. Internationalize the Panama Canal.

45. Repeal the Connally Reservation so the U.S. cannot prevent the World Court from seizing jurisdiction over domestic problems. Give the World Court jurisdiction over domestic problems. Give the World Court jurisdiction over nations and individuals alike.

About the Authors

Rev. Dale Witherington

As the Chief Steward of Restore Minnesota, Dale Witherington serves as a missionary/pastor to the elected officials, their families, and staff at the State Capitol in St. Paul, MN, as an educator to the church regarding the church's role in government, and to Minnesota's BPOUs to support the Constitutional collaboration between the government and the church. Dale and his team are planting Community Action Teams (CATs) and launching Institutes for Biblical Citizenship© in every county in Minnesota (and beyond as the Lord opens those doors), assisting the body of Christ in understanding its role as a maker of disciples who are engaged, biblical citizens. Together we are re-forming the church to transform the world.

Dale and his wife, Sue, have been married since December 1975. They have raised three sons and one daughter, who have blessed them with seven awesome grandchildren. They reside near the Twin Cities metro area.

Restore Minnesota (RestoreMN.org) exists to restore righteousness in Minnesota by promoting Biblical citizenship that educates, equips, empowers, and encourages Holy Spirit-led engagement—county by county, community by community, and family by family—resulting in spiritual and civic transformation based on the life and teachings, death and resurrection of the Lord Jesus Christ.

Pastor Dan Montague

Dan spent 48 years in secular employment while serving the Lord in many church leadership and teaching roles. He always knew in his heart there was more so he took the step of being ordained as a Pastor by his church a few years ago. He also became a Licensed Minister with International Ministerial Fellowship prior to October 2021, when he retired from the marketplace and stepped into the leadership team with Restore Minnesota as a Senior Steward.

He and his wife, Barb, essentially became missionaries to Minnesota to help restore righteousness to this great state through grassroots engagement that brings both spiritual and civic transformation. They pioneered the Sherburne County Community Action Team (CAT) in Elk River, MN in April 2021 and continue to assist in the startup and growth of more CATs.

Dan and his wife, Barb, live 20 minutes northwest of the Twin Cities metro area. Their remarried family now includes 22 grandchildren and 7 great grandchildren.